THE
TURTLE DOVE
TOLD ME

THE TURTLE DOVE TOLD ME

THANDI SLIEPEN

First published by Modjaji Books (Pty) Ltd 2013
PO Box 385, Athlone, 7760, Cape Town, South Africa
www.modjajibooks.co.za

Cover artwork by Thandi Sliepen
Book and Cover Design by Megan Ross
Editor: Kobus Moolman

Printed and bound by Megadigital, Cape Town
ISBN: 978-1-920590-48-2

Set in Garamond

Some of the poems have appeared in earlier versions in the following publications:
New Contrast, New Coin and *Commontatta.*

Dedicated to Martin Wessels, artist and unorthodox mentor.

'Martin's place' in Clarens was a sanctuary for many people over the years. A place of nature, creative freedom, Martin's visionary art and indomitable personality. It was a great gift.

CONTENTS

DESERT

SEA

CAVE

CITY

WINGS

-DESERT-

guava sunset

on a journey
suspended from before
or behind
just this taut
cord road
linking glimpses
filling my eyes as fast
as they drain away
just these watermarks
ringing our palms and feet
threaded with rose quartz

the sun dripping
away at dusk
to bubble up at dawn
the road
stretching away like elastic
resuming its shape
after you pass
the past
relaxing back into stone

the way

an ochre seam
lined with terracotta screens
elephant grass twice the height
of a woman

my famished road
where people materialize
in the red tunnel a man
in an ancient preacher suit

a woman with a baby
slung on her back
the breathing bundle in a boldly
patterned wrapper

a travelling salesman bent double
under an awkward rainbow
of plastic containers
heavy balloons in the dust

charcoal peddlers hauling
forgotten forests
transporting dry black waters everything
stacked on black bikes

chickens bounce by
like fluffed up cotton in wicker cages
pigs swing past wearing their
individually woven carrier bags

a man trying to flag me down
waving a red goats leg
a bunch of bananas
propped on a chair

piles of watermelon like
piles of carefully sorted greenstone
buckets of sweet potatoes
purple and cream

the road one long shop front
where people surface

like mushrooms
through the iron earth

a lone woman
centred in her kanga
exquisite faded fabric
a bowl on a hip

a man swinging his arms
so many styles
of walking
on this red river track

where visions
slip out the window
and are left by the roadside forever
the way passes me by

the desert

you walked alone
barefoot exile in vast
lime sulphur seas
and found there
no perspective
you can fit your home town
in the corner of one eye
as you walk away

but found also soldiering on
with a bleeding shadow
dripping over sand
and so returned to cultivated fields
that ward off those dry skies

a ploughing immigrant
in a promised land
but your children forget
wandering in dimly lit tv streets
with cushioned feet

i followed your trail here
into the heart of the desert
to stamp off
those false gods we nest in
the dust is brighter here
than i imagined

dar es salaam

haven of peace
how your inhabitants appear
like threads
in a well worn carpet
of faiths

for everyone a place
and space on the pavement
if your one leg is shrivelled and small
you can still walk in dar es salaam
if you have a basket of oranges
and a knife
you have a steady job
on the boulevard

there you are combing
rind off fruit
holding out two bowls in your hands
in a sheaf of time
in dar es salaam
where the rich eat ice cream
on the skyline
up a marble stairwell and dance
in discos with smoke machines

where stowaways
land between travels
and sleep in the rotund hulls
of the great wooden dhows
pulled ashore for repair
stowaways who will leap down
from their vessels
take you out for tea
and talk to you about poverty

the women with steel necks

do you walk
miles for water
the earth fuelling your beauty
through the dry cracks
and moulded arch of your soles

the women with steel necks
are passing
faded plastic buckets
are passing turning
around cool liquid bricks
as heads revolve to laugh and joke
retracing steps
in an endless curved landscape
anguine passage between
thighs land and sky

to know the weight
of every drop
precious pillars of salt
the women
with steel necks are passing

nymbamungu

i cast out
some seeds
like a net
in a conscious attempt to grasp
myself
or accidentally
followed by years of trawling
endless fingering of sea
through swirling green weed
and drowned hair
to find
one day standing
on an ebbing desert expanse
by any street corner
the setting sun facing a full moon
they come masses
of gasping flipping fish
in nymbamungu
at my feet

in the meantime

trying to stay awake
a cripple
a blind man and
three children
are naked in the water
a few passersby stop
to watch us splashing

-SEA-

now me heads

are stretching apart
reflections in an intercape
double bubble plastic bus
but i take
the free drink

blurred water joints
ductile fontanels
sticking together
i am hanging from the ceiling
every turn and glance outside
spilling the fake fruit juice
sucking me brains ever thinner
sinewy connections

flying guillotines
its a warning
gliding past white houses
overseeing white beaches
broken necks absurdly strolling
in severed tranquillity
onward on this journey of separation
wearing our shades
away from the bleached bays
a dip in the tarmac
all the heads in rows slip grip
only just remaining attached

inland the passing township
kids so far from the sea
superimposed on our hidden heads
a synthetic pane screening today
splitting bodies on
carved up land

new south africa

and they tell me of this land
that the signs have just come down
now only
no trespassers
no hawkers
no squatters
no loitering
no houses
no services
no work

and they tell me of this land
that the signs have just come down

capetown

walking through the traffic
with a guitar man suffering
from withdrawal symptoms along
with all his brothers and sisters
as the train preacher holding
a bible demands our salvation
the baby birds have fallen
from the nest going up
in smoke like buttons
crowds sucked past like streamers
from a departing cruise ship
as seen on the love boat
or a distant memory
of fanfare and stretching
snapping paper ribbons

the coloured women in the street
selling fruit are gossiping
calling out
where are your shoes
do you think you are sexy
another says to her friends
no man look she is happy

oma cloud

three tender footed ladies
wearing identical fabric print
went by one day like a cloud
with three heads

the three ladies holding hands
share limbs
oma it was your legs we used
mother and i with our
tender skin gloves

the same blue eyes gazing uneasily
down the communal well
oma the mirror you cried into
and taught your children to fear
has run dry

has become a warm pouch
for our bones picked clean
bleached and shuffled like sand
they were only the bones
i used
you and mother are free
and i am going sailing

she sells sea shells

on the sea shore
and plastic fish mobiles
that hang from her sun umbrella
garish fish that wildly tug
in the levitating air
while the storks inland
glide in afternoon columns
supporting a marble sky

she sells sea shells
on the sea shore
her dog has a blind eye
and keeps her company
while the holiday makers
come to buy

she finds the colours
sweetest when first picked
but then fade
in her fruit basket
her blind companion
counts the takings
while the plastic fish go
flying into the salty spray
combed off the waves

three companions

on a deserted coastline
running across our eyes
waves vibrating
between us
washing up oysters
we eat every day
and a young octopus
changing colour
sucking your fingers
even when dead
three companions
and a heron
watching from the dunes
its heavy wings
bending like spoons

our flapping mobiles
of driftwood and shell
go nowhere
knocking
outside the open door
of the wooden shack
we found
and the octopus lay
on that shipwrecked table
bloodshot
in the candlelight
three companions and i
drifting silently by
like ghost ships
each in our own way

taking turns to behold
our ambassador
from the rocky shore
on a flickering altar
still sucking our fingers
glazed black eyes
and there
a surge
of recognition

we are different

i do not play
the way you do
home in the water
i float on the skin
while you plough
rhythmically

the heron

on a crest of a dune
stands above the sand
and says
things look different today
not so grainy
as in over enlarged
photographs
lonely circles of silver
i see said the heron
where you stay quiet and why

amandla

in a forest where
the sun has just come out
pine needles line a golden underworld
outside the demonstration can still be heard
a distant sea of song or cloud
floating by i hear amandla
in a forest where yellowwoods grow

and the demonstration can still be heard
an ebbing tide from the valley below
returning in waves to where i sit
hearing my own voice come in
with the passing swell
or with the red-winged lourie or
with the wailing man
sitting next to me like a minstrel
outside the castle gates

the sun is sinking
soon the parade will be home
the birds tuned
to the silence of the night
though there is still a glow
it will be colder before dawn
the minstrel keeps watch

-CAVE-

art

matted hair a
yellow felt cap
like a half moon
shading my mind
just looking to survive
unstable ground i
snag in overgrown gardens
though the mornings are
full of birds swimming
inside my ears

blue overalls

the woman in the big house
down the road
with a new tin shed
as big as a bed
is screaming
at her gardener

the woman in the big house
is talking to her gnome
in blue overalls
in the garden
the woman in the big house
keeps gnomes in her shed

walking down the road
heading into town
i notice them everywhere
in every yard
blue overalls
as predictable as square lawns
and tightly pruned
rosebushes

walking back along the road
past the woman in the big house
past a kindly old gentleman
in blue overalls
i sink
into the perfumed air

two companions

she sent them on their way
with an apple each to eat
both said they would save the fruit
till morning
all were limping
with worm riddled
red material goods
to lord over and sell
for profit and fame

better to sit alone
than be tossed around
the room full of fearful
opinions i put some money down
walk out and watch
a fire cradling a pot
dying down a full moon
rises and sets
better to await the sun
each day than hunt warmth
from forgetful blood
so she sent them on their way
with an apple each to eat
both said they would save
the fruit till morning

we can see as clearly with the sun
as we can with the moon
when it is full and comes
inside the cave
two eyes on the same face
one watching ambivalently
the other opening and closing
like an eyelid
to a candlelit room

the moon will be full
before running out of sky
so she sent them on their way
with an apple each to eat
both said they would save
the fruit till morning

full moon in the cave

i am living a lifetime
desires in my heart an anchor
to this shore in a nest
that resembles a boat
you see a baby bird floating
with its beak up to the sky
like a pink party hat
calling to be fed

full moon in the cave
i am living a lifetime
desires in my heart an anchor
to this shore in a nest
or waning moon basket
in the rushes
bobbing the waves

full moon in the cave
i am living a lifetime
desires in my heart an anchor
to the shore my party
hat still waving

the mother of the calf

has been found
we followed her prints
up the hill in the morning
by dusk
she was found
still standing
but mute
not a word passed
from her lips
not a breath of welcome
for her young

we sang her praises
the old shepherd and i
asking what kind of land
she had seen
from her lookout
on the top of the hill
why she had deserted us

with a creaking sway
of her hips she offered
    her gaze
    her firstborn
    her milk
    her body
  her fresh tracks
on the eroded slope

she gave a dry smile
and followed us home
not a breath of welcome
for her young

song for moona

how does it feel
to be the slaughtered one
to be washed up
on a shore of hungry ones
to be washed up
into the hands of sleepwalkers
who have forgotten
your words
how does it feel
to be the sacrificed one
to be washed up in a crowd
of broken shells
and the blood on the stone
is your very own

i know what you must feel
i know what must be felt
you must love us a great deal
you must love us an arm
and a leg
to be the slaughtered one

so farewell to you
may you find
peace of mind
may you feel your blood
was well spent
may you one day discover
you can bless the sleepwalkers
and the sky

the engagement party

with an absence of faith
she warms her back
against the sun or
spit braai
as a pig rolls over
in a crisp skin
soaked in two bottles of oil
celebrating their cravings
she watches couples
swarm the meat

with an absence of faith
smiling in a white shirt
like a bemused angel
she leaves the tables
unturned
enjoying the heat and crackle
of the scene

occasionally whispering
brothers and sisters
we must start
to untangle
the flesh from our teeth
like a train preacher
in the first carriage
the fervour of movement
still dormant
or lack of faith
tanning her back

waiting for your return

in a pool of light
with streaming water
and dogs in the distance barking
like two voices from an old
bitter womans throat
waiting for your return
by a glittering fireside
a pink candy roof
under a bruised purple sky
i hear tales of empires
that come and go
a war torn forest
tales from an artist
full of frames
each word from an old
bitter womans throat
flickering orange tongues
dancing over sticky walls
i see mothers handing
their daughters ribs
newly born given gristly
dummies to suck
and we think this is a house
in a forest or
the sweetmeat vendor
has set up shop
as parents wander off
disappearing into trees
not able to show their affection
crushing the trail of bread
i wait for another
i wait for everyone
waiting for your return
to replace the voice
of running water and
dogs in the distance barking
to replace the voice
eating away at itself
doves live in the cave

the holkrans

i am a temporary guardian
of this cave
on moonlit nights
i write in the light
and listen to birds
bats and a dripping tap
i study a cascade of algae
riddles and shadows
a family of faces
in the rock

like a blossoming tree
bearing fruit
shedding skin then
moving on
weary travellers berth in this cave
that resembles a harbour
birds sail
amongst the clouds
floating seaweed in the sky
at dusk bats
like escaping curtains from
this round blue window
leave to return at dawn

the more homes
that have welcomed me
pile up harbours behind
and sailors who took me
closer to the sea will sail off
in their own vessels
and i will let them
go

old man

growing old
like burnt veld
going grey
then green
again

-CITY-

dogs lament

the city echoes
a dogs lament

through human streets
i must go

clown city

welcome
welcome
welcome child
how could we miss the chance
to welcome you

newcomer to the streets
walk on
walk on
walk on
i present to you enlightenment centres
full of fold out maps
when to clap
whom to watch
where to dine
what to buy
welcome to the shoe shop

wear your swollen feet
painted face
welcome to clown city
a life of ushering in cars
plenty of parking
but nowhere to sleep

watch the tent
watch the tent
watch the tent
it is going under
like a deep sea turtle
with nowhere to land or safely
lay her eggs

frankas village

hosts my burning home
tonight mine workers
those who are
above ground
will see their lives
and ask are we not still
children were we not born
under a wide sky or during
a cool rain

and the actors will look
straight into their eyes
the dancers shower joy
the drums will call
and keep their souls
from her black hole
heart

happy moles

sons and brothers deserting the sun
for weak fluorescent lights
every fifty metres a false dawn

how do you grow
mole through these new
umbilical cords
your navel bleeds
mole where is your mother
tell her snakes run
out of gods garden
and feed you
under a plastic moon hard hat
hiding you
as if you were made for the dark
and never walked the earth
mole are you happy
your face still beams your
first fresh breaths
your skin black
with the blessing of the sun
the blue sky
your birthright
all day all night
mole have you deserted us

this is your time in the sun
let your blood flow
out of the tunnels
that were never yours
how are your eyes mole
your ringing ears
is it worth anything
for anyone this burrowing
away from the light

the hyena and the lion

i saw them on tv
life is fickle
laughed
the hyena to the lion
as she pricked her finger
and mixed her blood
on the lions
bleeding paw

as the crowd cries
shoot us
the police shift from
foot to foot wishing
they were back
in their mothers arms

tonight i will kill
your children
said the lion
to the hyena
and leave you their bodies
in the dust
covered in an old coat

then i must mourn
said the hyena and she began
to spin gold
chasing her tail
chewing
her red stained teeth

time of the dogs

morning dog bark
over the land
a wave of mourning
a predawn procession the torch
passing between our fences
from coast to coast
dark city to dark city
a wave of wailing
our pain calling
unchained in the dark
i thought i heard the voice
of chaos but
it was only the time of the dogs
washing over the land
before the roosters calling
randomly for the sun

the waste land

how can anything grow
with no blue sky above
how can we uproot and lay
to waste our days

the gold reef is shattered
gone is our ease
the land trembles under
explosions or a stampede

in this city of cage homes
and red sunsets
where our bones feed
the wasteland

one day like elephants
we will have to reclaim
them these bones of our body
to be done

take away this scene
this city is a place of blindness
and fragmented visions
take away my bones

-WINGS-

surrender hill

i have come to a house where
an anchor welcome mat lies
on the sandstone stoep
and a fallen weavers nest
through an open sky
blue door
down a cool corridor
stagnant rooms on
either side where people
sleep and breathe
looking out of
sky blue windows

i have come to a tower
as a woman gives birth
going insane
and back again
to the sound of sheep moving
on surrender hill

i leave the stone mansion
behind where doves in the rafters
follow you from room to room
and the white horse is always
just outside the window
i leave coerland
over the slippery black lichen
to the summit of shrapnel

past the bare patches of earth
where nothing will grow
past the spider cities draped in dew
suspension bridges
flashing at dawn

past the memorial plaque
into the assembly of flying insects
and travelling seeds
to the fading sound of sheep moving
on surrender hill

school

the children are running
to school barefoot
through the mist
hot tarmac
gravelly stones
smooth clay
children running
with fragile exercise book
wrapped in plastic bag
for miles
the children are running
all over africa

the quiet ones

moon ceiling
sunrise door
opening onto a graveyard
i have seen tolkiens hobbits
they stand like old sandstone fence posts
amongst tall thatching grasses
under sandstone cliffs
caves in hills that floor the sky

look for the quiet ones
you will dream peacefully
by their side
or they will walk along the road
with you returning home
their faces still hidden their hearts
of stone are not easily swayed
will tell you we are all cast
from the light
like passing shadows over the earth

in her bright yellow house
a sunflower path leading away
she works through the night
on a kite that need not fly
in fields of poisonous berries
if she speaks
she will describe sweet red fruits
and the ships she is searching for
and the harbour
where they berth all going
east she is thinking about the east
like a leaning statue
at dusk
waiting for the tide
houses soon flooded by sand
they are leaving
the quiet ones

middle earth not a
holiday resort to linger
in all summer

the field

there are strawberries i want to save
but there is no time
i count the hours like rows
of severed fruit
and elephant hearts
the day passes
a pulse of ringing bells
oma those last days
all you could eat were strawberries

a new south african flag is flying
over the lombardy poplars
above our village
a lone piet my vrou is calling
in the night
the weaver birds treading light
threading their hanging gardens
as i dream we are waiting
for the lion
to swallow the sun

in the heat haze i see the garden
that could be
each fork full a burden
and a blessing
if i dig deep i touch the black marrow
the basement clay of this valley
i think we all have our own fields to dig
the kind of field
no gardener can dig for you
our own beds to make
to lie in
no maid can straighten

a new south african flag is flying
over the weeping willows
above our village
there is no moon
orange butterflies dance
around the blue skirts of the dams
as the old strawberry plants lie discarded
in the dust

the caves cup the air
like the ears of the land
inquisitively listening
to us
to the sounds of our names
to the hadedas passing overhead
like the remnants of prehistoric birds
trumpeting like old men
who have just learnt to fly
to wake us
our fields are standing

ou werf

all the turtles
are flying to the moon
martin do you see them
once you gave me a cave
to live in and now
you are like the ferryman
to the land of cadmium
lemon hue

all the turtles
are leaving i see them
silhouetted wings in the sky
and you so stern
now i pray may i see
wings on all our
ancient backs

pigeons on the road

they will move on
the pigeons on the road
returning only to gather in
those left behind
as the flock does a final
arc in the sky
through an open door the shepherd
leans reabsorbing stragglers
like a whirlwind lifting
light waters into his fold
they will move on
the pigeons on the road
after satisfying their hunger
on grain that fell
like rain after the harvest
they will move on
and leave no one behind

reunion

people have been talking about you all day
with affection
speculating on your return
reminding me with talk of photographs
dark rooms
and the enlarger they say
you would have been able to fix

i have been visiting your old friends
and bathing in essential oils
candlelight and ylang-ylang
gazing out of a misted well
at the mermaid woman
i have just painted
on their bathroom ceiling

waiting for a familiar love
to return home laden with gifts
from distant lands
frankincense and myrrh
a satellite passes overhead
as i dream my teeth fall out one by one
and a familiar love
returns home

you and me under the syringa tree

the bats are swooping
parcels of free floating night
we are talking in twilight
under the syringa tree

a spray of muted
purple stars above
ringing voices overflow
from the still well of the air
children calling in the dusk
stretching their days
into night

we breathe the sounds
and drink the air
on a carpet of fallen petals
like autumn leaves
rearranging in the wake
of our prancing feet

a dance my love
a dance coming round
and round again
our eyes lock as we part

and there my fear
you see
bloating my heart
that you will spin away
a lifetime alone
under the syringa tree

the riverbed

remember the eland
in golden gate
i woke to
outside our tent
pale and curious

and the same eland again
driving past the city zoo
walking a different ridge
at sunset

years have past
they pass like pages
in my heart

remember how we walked
up the dry riverbed
and found an old leather harness
and the bones of a horse
like charred roots
embedded into layers
of flooded years

years have past
they pass
my heart a red river
running into a red sea

remember how we walked
up the mountain
past the wild olive tree
and heard the baboons
crying from their towers

remember how you
and i reached the summit
and lay on the overhang
like angels on a cloud
looked down onto
the golden field
that birthed us
that holds our gravestones

a field bathed in light

years have past
they pass like moths
imprisoned in my hands
i must set free
when i reach the top

the turtle dove told me

fly on
fearful one
the world is full of beauty
where ever you may find it
move on
cling not to these sandstone mountains
this high dry air
welcome change

Other Poetry Titles by Modjaji Books

Fourth Child by Megan Hall
Life in Translation by Azila Talit Reisenberger
Please, Take Photographs by Sindiwe Magona
Burnt Offering by Joan Metelerkamp
Strange Fruit by Helen Moffett
Oleander by Fiona Zerbst
The Everyday Wife by Phillippa Yaa de Villiers
missing by Beverly Rycroft
These are the lies I told you by Kerry Hammerton
Conduit by Sarah Frost
The Suitable Girl by Michelle McGrane
Piece Work by Ingrid Andersen
Difficult Gifts by Dawn Garisch
Woman Unfolding by Jenna Mervis
removing by Melissa Butler
At least the Duck Survived by Margaret Clough
Bare & Breaking by Karin Schimke
The Reckless Sleeper by Haidee Kruger
Beyond the Delivery Room by Khadija Heeger